Tenth Edition

INTERNATIONAL ECONOMICS

A POLICY APPROACH

Mordechai E. Kreinin
Michigan State University

THOMSON
⋆
SO**U**TH-WESTERN

Australia • Canada • Mexico • Singapore • Spain • United Kingdom • United States

THOMSON
SOUTH-WESTERN

International Economics: A Policy Approach, Tenth Edition
Mordechai E. Kreinin

VP/Editorial Director:
Jack W. Calhoun

VP/Editor-in-Chief:
Dave Shaut

Editor-in-Chief:
Alex von Rosenberg

Developmental Editor:
Jennifer E. Baker

Sr. Marketing Manager:
John Carey

Production Project Manager:
Brian Courter

Manager of Technology, Editorial:
Vicky True

Production Technology Project Manager:
Peggy Buskey

Web Coordinator:
Karen L. Schaffer

Sr. Manufacturing Coordinator:
Sandee Milewski

Production House:
International Typesetting
and Composition

Printer:
Quebecor World Taunton
Taunton, MA

Art Director:
Michelle Kunkler

Cover and Internal Designers:
Design Matters
Cincinnati, OH

Cover Images:
© Getty Images

Library of Congress Control Number:
2005926900

For more information about our
products, contact us at:

Thomson Learning Academic
Resource Center
1-800-423-0563

Thomson Higher Education
5191 Natorp Boulevard
Mason, OH 45040
USA